T0294312

NATURE

NATURE

Mark Truscott

BookThug | *MMX*

FIRST EDITION

copyright © Mark Truscott, 2010

The production of this book was made possible through
the generous assistance of The Canada Council for The
Arts and The Ontario Arts Council.

 Canada Council   Conseil des Arts
for the Arts   du Canada

 ONTARIO ARTS COUNCIL
CONSEIL DES ARTS DE L'ONTARIO

All rights reserved. No part of this publication may be
reproduced or transmitted in any form or by any means,
electronic or mechanical, including photocopying,
recording, or any information storage or retrieval system,
without permission in writing from the publisher.

Printed in Canada.

LIBRARY AND ARCHIVES CANADA
CATALOGUING IN PUBLICATION

Truscott, Mark, 1970 –
           Nature / Mark Truscott.
Poems.
ISBN 978‑1‑897388‑67‑9
           I. Title.
PS8639.R88N38 2010   C811'.6   C2010‑905581‑0

for Sam and Lucy

Nature is the hint to composition not because it is familiar to us and therefore the terms we apply to it have a least common denominator quality which gives them currency — but because it possesses the quality of independent existence, of reality which we feel in ourselves. It is not opposed to art but apposed to it.

— William Carlos Williams

NATURE

one
or
a
non

one
o
one
on

no
one
on
one

The last
word

was the
first.

EDGE

ninety nine one hundred

INFINITY

one

two

six

ten

FORM

These

two

words

if branches
s branch

A bird sings a
letter hangs in the balance

SQUARE

which is
which is

BODY

One meets one
on the line
one is on.

RAPTURE

The line or quote the
line, been there.

TREMBLER

out of a
loud soft hat

an n on

a door

on and on toward and on

and and and and and this and

and and and and and this end

It's like it's going to try to run it.

so
forth

four

one

one

one

two

one
wall

one
floor

One two
and one
more.

Things
fall
where
they
may.

air
around
rings
around
from
around
hills
around

The a
sticks.

A the
on the
floor.

Black white.
Grey green.
A marvel.

yellow circle
blue circle
brown circle
green circle
red circle
orange circle
purple circle

(NOTHING FUCKING)
FUCKING NOTHING

The
The word
The word the
The word the phrase
The word the phrase starts
The word the phrase starts with

There
There is
There is there
There is there is
There is there is there

flying out
absolute
flies out

the relative

– Thomas A. Clark

one two
three four
five six
seven eight
nine ten

logic or
form in
g hell
but won't
look up

this word
points to
that shows
connection and
apes it

that this
is the
one that
is on
that page

that that
is the
one that
is on
this page

that that
that that
that that
that one
sells down

up here
and it's
right there
on the
top now

the brick
shows the
force to
slow choice
to stack

an edge
here and
one here
and still
others too

I wonder
if the
space this
creates will
hold it

a drop
falls the
surface that
catches it
fills in

where oh
this one
no it's
no there
it is

the range
of kerning
or adjectival
curing space
close it

if one

were to

mean one's

were to

if one

hit of
hat it
have it
hide it
hold it

it's like

it says

its own

it sows

its shoes

do you
still have
it no
I don't
anymore you

what if
the words
were to
be set
off kilter

then the
grid would
bleed and
the thatch
shine out

and the
sun shine
beams fuck
the ledge
is cold

words among
these be
this thing
here say
and here

not not

one not

one not

one one

not one

one six
ten two
five four
nine eight
seven three

This, here.

I think
elsewhere.

No (correction), not
really.

This, here, or
more

like
her.

Here or
here on
the most
like itself
pill bug

No, not

note

it's

mute.

The thing
curls

and
talks.

quiet

quite

raining

ESSAYS ON NATURE

in the
interstice
that this
can't enter
a deictic
room tone
hums

these words

stay these

solid lines

force

or

form

or

one

or

more

a word
to mark
where the
thought begins
to falter

a word
to mark
where the
thought begins
to form

the word
that occurs
where a
thought begins
to falter

the word
that occurs
where a
thought begins
to form

these words
that abut
a thought
that starts
to falter

these words
that abut
a thought
that starts
to form

ACKNOWLEDGEMENTS

Thanks to Marianne Apostolides, Louis Cabri, Kevin Connolly, Dianne Cowan, Thomas Evans, Lisa Heggum, Lisa Jarnot, Donato Mancini, Jay MillAr, Bill Minor, Jenny Sampirisi, Jordan Scott, Ron Silliman, Stacy Szymaszek, Alana Wilcox, and Rachel Zolf.

Poems in *Nature* have previously appeared in *1Cent, Peter O'Toole,* and *Xerography,* and on the *Ditch* and Delirium Press websites.

The poem on page 22 was co-written by Sam Heggum-Truscott.

Thanks to the Ontario Arts Council for two Writers' Reserve grants.

COLOPHON

Manufactured in an edition of 500 copies
in the fall of 2010. Distributed in Canada
by The Literary Press Group: www.lpg.ca.
Distributed in the United States by Small
Press Distribution: www.spdbooks.org.
Shop online at www.bookthug.ca

BOOK
PRODUCTION
WAR ECONOMY
STANDARD

Type + Design by Jay MillAr